# Le Mot Juste

## How to Impress
## *Tout le Monde* with
## your French

Imogen Fortes

Michael O'Mara Books Limited

First published in Great Britain in 2018 by
Michael O'Mara Books Limited
9 Lion Yard
Tremadoc Road
London SW4 7NQ

A CIP catalogue record for this book is available from the British Library.

Papers used by Michael O'Mara Books Limited are natural, recyclable products
made from wood grown in sustainable forests. The manufacturing processes
conform to the environmental regulations of the country of origin.

An immense merci and my heartfelt gratitude to the French cohorts and
Parisian chums who have inspired, contributed or cast their eye over this
collection: Jeni Carlisle, Sylvie Brandl, Patrick Clargé and Benjamin Lefebure.
And with thanks to Polly Bennett and Nina Sivyer for the reflections from this
side of the Channel - the pamplemousse made it in...

ISBN: 978-1-78243-986-8 in hardback print format
ISBN: 978-1-78243-987-5 in ebook format

1 2 3 4 5 6 7 8 9 10

Design and illustration by Jade Wheaton
Printed and bound in Malta

www.mombooks.com

# Introduction

The French language is many things. For the French, it is a revered and precious possession: an asset they take enormous pride in and one they fight tooth and nail to protect from the marching invasion of the anglicisms and the 'franglais' threatening to blight and decay its sanctity and purity.

For foreigners, French generally falls into one of two camps. To learners of the language, it can be the stuff of nightmares – the bane of school days, responsible for countless hours spent wrestling with pronouns, trying to make sense of its conjugations or pronounce its wretched throaty 'r's. And then there are the admirers: those of us who will never fail to be charmed by its elegance and seduced by its melody and grace.

This book is for them all: it is a celebration of the beauty and romance found in the Gallic turn of phrase; yet it is also a tool – a guide to making your way through the charming, delicious, seductive and wonderful world of French culture, and adding your own *mot juste* to a *tête-a-tête*, a romantic *rendez-vous*, an exchange of opinion or just an everyday chat with a chum.

# Des Mots en Harmonie

## Words in Harmony

French is the language of Molière, Duras and Flaubert: a complex yet elegant tongue, it is full of sensual sounds and mellifluous turns of phrase. But it's no coincidence that French often sounds like a melody. The French have an ardent dedication to 'euphony' – the quality of sounding harmonious – and French speakers abide by strict rules to ensure those soft, breathy vowels and gentle liaisons come together in a beautiful song. It's the stuff of nightmares for learners, but the result never fails to charm a foreign ear.

In this chapter you'll find some of the words and phrases that showcase the beauty and rigour of the French language.

# Une belle âme

[ewn behl am]

## A good person
(literally, a beautiful soul)

# Chuchoter

[shoo-sho-tay]

## To whisper

# Un nuage

[ahn new-azh]

A cloud

# À la folie

[a lah fol-ee]

## Madly

# Un tête-à-tête

[ahn tet-a-tet]

A one-to-one
discussion

# Un pamplemousse

[ahn pom-pleu-mousse]

A grapefruit

# Une hirondelle

[ewn ee-rohn-dehl]

A swallow

DES MOTS EN HARMONIE

# Une noisette

[ewn noo-wah-zet]

A hazelnut

# Un parapluie

[ahn pa-ra-ploowee]

## An umbrella

# Un chou-fleur

[ahn shoo-flur]

## A cauliflower

# Un loup-garou

[ahn loo-ga-roo]

A werewolf

# Inoubliable

[ee-noo-blee-ab-leu]

## Unforgettable

# Un papillon

[ahn pa-pee-yon]

A butterfly or a bowtie

# À la louche

[a lah loosh]

## Approximately
(literally, using a ladle)

# À couper le souffle

[a coo-pay luh soof-leu]

Breathtaking

# Un flocon de neige

[ahn flok-ohn duh nezh]

## A snowflake

# Fais de beaux rêves

[fay d'boh rev]

Sweet dreams

# S'évader

[say-va-day]

To escape

# Une pantoufle

[ewn pohn-too-fleu]

## A slipper

# Un mouton

[ahn moo-tohn]

A sheep

# Flâner

[fla-nay]

To wander without
purpose

# Au clair de lune

[oh clare duh lewn]

In the moonlight

# Le bonheur

[luh boh-ner]

Happiness

# Une étoile

[ewn ay-twahl]

A star

# Une lueur d'espoir

[ewn loo-er des-pwahr]

A glimmer of hope

# Larmes de joie

[larm duh zhwah]

Tears of joy

# Adieu

[a-dyeu]

Farewell

# Vivre Pleinement l'instant Présent

Living Life to the Full

Long, leisurely lunches; lingering over a morning coffee; a stroll around a market or the smell of a baguette still warm from the oven – the French have long been praised for their joie de vivre, their passionate zest for life.

This chapter encapsulates that quintessential French spirit with the words and phrases the French use to express their desire to seize the day, truly live in the moment and celebrate the beauty and joy in life's simple pleasures. From the inspirational to the practical, these are sentiments we could perhaps all do with embracing in order to live our own lives to their fullest.

# La joie de vivre

[lah zhwah duh vee-vreu]

## A zest for life

(literally, the joy of living)

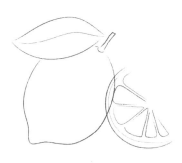

# Je ne regrette rien

[juh nuh ruh-gret-eu ree-yahn]

I regret nothing

# Croquer la vie
# à pleines dents

[croh-kay lah vee a plen don]

## To embrace life
## to its fullest

(literally, to bite into life with
all your teeth)

# Mangez bien, riez souvent, aimez beaucoup

[mahn-zhay bee-yahn, ree-yay soo-vahn, em-ay boh-coo]

Eat well, laugh often, love abundantly

# Comme il faut

[com eel foe]

As it should be

# C'est la vie

[say lah vee]

That's life

# L'amour l'emporte

[lah-moor lom-port]

## Love prevails

# Qui n'avance pas, recule

[ki nav-ahns pah, ruh-koo!]

If you don't move forwards, you move backwards

# Un bon vivant

[ahn bohn veev-ahn]

## A person who 'lives it up'

(literally, a good 'liver'; the phrase is
commonly used in the context of somebody
who likes to eat and drink well)

# La vie est trop courte pour boire du mauvais vin

[la vee ay trow cour-teu poor bwahr
doo mo-vay vahn]

## Life is too short to drink bad wine

# La vie en rose

[la vee ohn rowz]

## Life in rosy hues

'Plus tard ce sera trop tard. La vie c'est maintenant'

Jacques Prévert

[ploo tahr se se-rah trow tahr.
La vee say mahn-teu-nohn]

'Later will be too late.
Life is for living now'

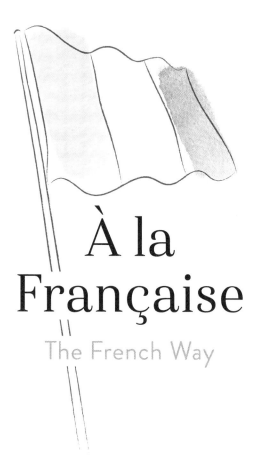

# À la Française

## The French Way

As a Romance language, French has few similarities to English. Understanding and translating it can be a challenge, to say the least, but its nuances reach even more complex heights when you attempt to untangle the bewildering world of the idiom.

This chapter takes you through some of the charming, perplexing, often downright baffling French phrases whose literal translation gives absolutely no hint as to the true meaning.

# Avoir la pêche

[av-wahr lah pesh]

## To be in high spirits

(literally, to have the peach)

# Tomber dans les pommes

[tom-bay dohn lay pomm-eu]

## To faint

(literally, to fall into the apples)

# C'est la fin des haricots

[say lah fahn day aree-kow]

## All is lost

(literally, it's the end of the green beans)

# Poser un lapin

[po-zay ahn la-pahn]

## To stand someone up
(literally, to place a rabbit)

# Appuyer sur le champignon

[a-pwee-yay syeur luh shom-pee-gnahn]

## To put your foot down
[on the car's accelerator]
(literally, to press on the mushroom)

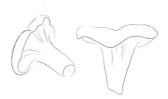

# Tu chantes du yaourt

[tuw shahn-teu doo ya-oor]

## You're making up the song lyrics

(literally, you're singing yoghurt)

# Faire la grasse matinée

[fair lah graz mat-ee-nay]

## To have a lie-in

(literally, to do the fat morning)

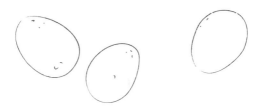

# Tondre des oeufs

[tohn-druh day zeugh]

## To be a cheapskate

(literally, to mow eggs)

# Sauter du coq à l'âne

[so-tay doo cok a lan]

## To change the subject abruptly
(literally, to jump from the cockerel to the donkey)

# Ça ne casse pas trois pattes à un canard

[sa nuh cass pah twah pat a ahn can-ar]

## It's nothing to write home about

(literally, it doesn't break
three of a duck's legs)

# En faire tout un fromage

[ohn fair toot ahn from-azh]

## To make a fuss

(literally, to make a whole
cheese out of it)

# Raconter des salades

[rak-ohn-tay day sa-lad-eugh]

## To tell lies

(literally, to tell salads)

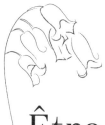

# Être fleur bleue

[et-reu flur bleugh]

## To be sentimental

(literally, to be a blue flower)

# Être comme un coq en pâte

[et-reu com ahn cok ohn pat]

## To feel cosy or pampered

(literally, to be like a cockerel in dough)

# Il me court sur le haricot

[eel muh coor syeur luh aree-kow]

## He's getting on my nerves

(literally, he's running on my bean)

# Une nostalgie de la boue

[ewn nos-tal-zhee duh lah boow]

A desire to live a simpler life/to downsize

(literally, a yearning for mud)

# Selon l'Auteur

In the Words of the Artist

France's intellectuals and artists have delighted, instructed and moved the world for centuries. In the words of some of the most famous among them are philosophies to inspire us all.

'Le bonheur est parfois caché dans l'inconnu'

Victor Hugo

[luh boh-ner ay par-fwah
ka-shay dohn lahn-kon-ew]

'Happiness is sometimes hidden
in the unknown'

'Ce qui est important,
c'est cette lumière
intérieure qui est en tous'

Jeanne Moreau

[se ki et am-pour-tahn, say seht loom-ee-air
ahn-tay-ree-yer-eu ki eht ohn toos]

'What is important is this internal
light which shines in all of us'

'Le seul vrai langage au monde est un baiser'

Alfred de Musset

[luh seughl vray long-gazh oh mahn-deu
et-ahn bay-zay]

'The only true language
in the world is a kiss'

'J'accepte la grande aventure d'être moi'

Simone de Beauvoir

[zhak-sept lah grahnd avohn-tyure det-reu mwah]

'I accept the great adventure
of being me'

'C'est cela l'amour, tout donner, tout sacrifier sans espoir de retour'

Albert Camus

[say se-lah lah-moor, toow donnay, toow sac-ree-fyay, sahn zes-pwahr duh reu-toor]

'That's what love is, to give everything, to sacrifice everything without hoping for anything in return'

'Du sublime au ridicule,
il n'y a qu'un pas'

Napoleon Bonaparte

[doo soo-bleem oh ree-dee-kewl,
eel nee-ya k-ahn pah]

'From the sublime to the ridiculous,
there is but one step'

'Rester, c'est exister, mais voyager, c'est vivre'

Gustave Nadaud

[ress-tay, say egg-sees-tay,
may vwah-ya-zhay, say vee-vreu]

'To stay is to exist,
but to travel is to live'

'Nous sommes
nos choix'

Jean-Paul Sartre

[noo som no shwah]

'We are our choices'

'Les commencements
ont des charmes
inexprimables'

Molière

[lay kom-ohns-mohn ohn day sharm-eu
ee-necks-pree-ma-bleugh]

'Beginnings have
inexplicable charms'

'Sans élégance de coeur,
il n'y a pas d'élégance'

Yves Saint Laurent

[sahn-zel-ay-gahns duh keur,
eel nee-ya pah del-ay-gahns]

'Without elegance of the
heart, there is no elegance'

'La beauté commence au moment où vous décidez d'être vous-même'

Coco Chanel

[lah boh-tay kom-ohns o mo-mahn oo voo day-see-day det-reu voo mem]

'Beauty begins the moment you decide to be yourself'

'Il est grand temps
de rallumer les étoiles.'

Guillaume Apollinaire

[eel ay grahn tom duh rall-oo-may
layz ay-twah!]

'It's time we lit up the stars again'

'Le monde est un livre dont chaque pas nous ouvre une page'

Alphonse de Lamartine

[luh mahn det-ahn lee-vreu, dahn shak pah nooz oo-vreu ewn pazh]

'The world is a book; with each step we open a fresh page'

'Il y a des fleurs partout pour qui veut bien les voir'

Henri Matisse

[eel ee ya day flur par-toow poor
ki veuh bee-yahn lay vwahr]

'There are flowers everywhere
for those who want to see them'

# L'Art de la Séduction

The Art of Seduction

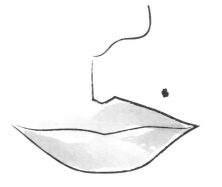

The French are masters of seduction. Everywhere you look, someone is trying to charm, beguile or even extricate themselves from a difficult situation using the subtle, persuasive power of seduction. For the French, seduction is as much in the gesture – a sultry look, a fleeting touch of the hand or a slight pout of the lips – as it is in the spoken word. But there is no doubt that the language of love will get you a long way towards conquering the object of your affection.

What follows is an insight into the phrases and words that will help you to navigate the mysterious, alluring, sensual and often confusing world of French romance and seduction.

# Le coup de foudre

[luh coo duh foo-dreugh]

## Love at first sight

(literally, a thunder bolt)

# Draguer

[dra-gay]

To flirt/chat somebody up

# Séduire

[sed-wee-reu]

To seduce

# Je peux vous offrir un verre?

[juh peuh voo-zoff-reer ahn vair]

Can I buy you a drink?

# Doux baisers

[Doow bay-zay]

## Tender kisses

# Embrasse-moi!

[om-brah-seu mwah]

Kiss me!

# J'ai le coeur qui bat la chamade

[zhay luh keur ki bah lah sha-mad]

## My heart is pounding

# Tomber amoureux

[tom-bay ah-moor-eugh]

To fall in love

-------------------------------

# T'as d'beaux yeux, tu sais

[tah d'bo-zyeh tuw say]

You have beautiful eyes, you know

# Je t'aime

[juh tem]

I love you

# Bisous volés

[bee-zoo vol-lay]

## Stolen kisses

# Un amour fou

[Uhn ah-moor foo]

## An uncontrollable passion

(literally, a mad love)

# Vivre une grande histoire d'amour

[vee-vrewn grahnd ee-stwahr dah-moor]

## To experience a great love affair

# Une douzaine de roses

[ewn doow-zen duh rowz]

A dozen roses

# Un amant

[Uhn-am-ohn]

## A lover

# Faire la cour

[Fair lah coor]

To seduce/court someone

# Une femme fatale

[Ewn fam fa-tahl]

## A dangerously/irresistibly seductive woman

(literally, a disastrous woman)

# On est fait l'un pour l'autre

[on ay fay lahn poor low-treu]

We're made for each other

# Je vis d'amour et d'eau fraîche

[juh vee dah-moor ay doh fresh]

## I'm surviving on love alone

(literally, I'm living on love and fresh water)

# Tu me manques

[too muh mahn-keu]

I miss you

# Reviens-moi

[ruh-vyahn mwah]

## Come back to me

# Les Beaux Arts

## The Arts

For centuries France has been a haven for writers, artists and performers. It is a nation where a love of the arts runs deep; where literature, painting, sculpture, music, dance, architecture, photography and film have flourished and left their mark on the country's history, identity and – perhaps most profoundly – on its people's chosen topics of conversation. The French can spend hours dissecting the director's cut of the latest film noir or scrutinizing the merits of a choreographer's artistic direction.

This chapter is your bluffer's guide to circumnavigating the often controversial, divisive world of French culture: arm yourself with these terms if ever you find yourself in the firing line when the French discuss the finer points of the arts.

# L'avant-garde

[la-vahn gar-deu]

New and experimental
ideas in the arts
(literally, a vanguard or front line)

# Le septième art

[luh seht-ee-yem ar]

## The cinema

(literally, the seventh art)

# Un personnage

[ahn pair-son-nazh]

A character

# Les beaux esprits se rencontrent

[lay boh-zess-pree se rohn-kohn-treu]

## The meeting
## of great minds

# Une librairie

[ewn leeb-rair-ee]

## A bookshop
(not a library)

# Une exposition

[ewn eks-poe-zee-syohn]

## An exhibition

# Un tableau

[ahn tab-low]

## A painting

# Une toile

[ewn twahl]

## A canvas

# Un coup de pinceau

[ahn coo duh pahn-sow]

## A brushstroke

# Une aquarelle

[ewn–ak–wa–rehl]

## A watercolour

# Un chef-d'œuvre

[ahn shay deu-vreu]

A masterpiece

# A découvrir absolument

[a day-coov-reer ab-sol-oo-mahn]

## Not to be missed

# Le décor

[luh day-cawr]

## The set/scenery
(in theatre)

# Un trompe-l'œil

[ahn trom-pleuy]

An artistic technique used to create
a visual illusion that tricks viewers
into thinking a painted object is real

(literally, a 'trick the eye')

# Son œuvre s'inspire de . . .

[son eu-vreu sahn-speer-eu duh]

His/her work
is inspired by . . .

# Le mot juste

[luh mow joost]

Exactly the right word

## 'Les livres sont des amis froids et sûrs'

Victor Hugo

[lay lee-vreu sahn dayz-amee frwah ay soor]

'Books are cold but sure friends'

# À Table

## To Sit Down at the Table

For the French, food is life. If they're not eating it, they're thinking about it, talking about it, shopping for it or planning it. This is, after all, the nation that invented the restaurant, where the cuisson of one's steak, the girth of a frite or the maturation point of a Camembert can divide families, and where wine is more important than water.

The table remains very much the heart of the French home, and the national cuisine, with its associated rituals and rhetoric, is something of which the French are immensely (and deservedly) proud. Pass over this chapter at your peril – it is a survival kit you are guaranteed to need on French soil.

-----------------------------

# La crème de la crème

[lah crem duh lah crem]

## The cream of the crop

(literally, the cream of the cream)

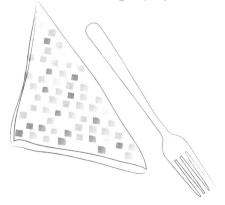

# Bon appétit!

[bohn-ap-eh-tee]

Enjoy your meal!

# Une amuse-bouche

[ewn ah-mooz-boosh]

## A bite-sized item of food served before a meal

(literally, something amusing for the mouth)

# Hors-d'œuvre

[awr d'eu–vreu]

A pre-meal snack
(literally, 'outside the work', i.e.
not part of the main serving)

# Un petit-four

[ahn puh-tee-foor]

A bite-sized dessert or
piece of confectionary
(literally, a little oven)

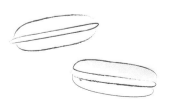

# Avoir de la bouteille

[av-wahr duh lah boo-tay-eu]

The value, experience and wisdom that one gains with age
(literally, having some bottle)

# Un(e) gourmand(e)

[uhn goor-mahnewn-de(u)]

Someone who enjoys their food

# Saucer

[sow-say]

To soak up the sauce left
on your plate with bread

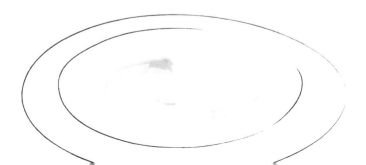

# Boire comme un trou

[bwar com ahn truw]

## To drink heavily

(literally, to drink like a hole)

# Avoir un petit creux

[av-wahr ahn puh-tee creugh]

## To feel peckish

(literally, to have a little hollow)

# Avoir la dalle

[av-wahr lah dal]

## To be starving

(literally, to have a paving stone)

# Faire sauter

[fair so-tay]

To fry something quickly
in a little oil or butter
(literally, to make something leap)

# Un en-cas

[ah-nohn-ka]

A snack

(literally, a 'just in case')

# Prendre un apéro

[prohn-dr ahn ap-eh-row]

To go for pre-dinner drinks and nibbles (a French ritual)

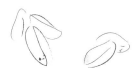

# Je suis repu(e)

[juh swee re-puw]

## I'm full

(I'm replete)

# La bouffe

[lah boof]

Grub/nosh

# Cordon bleu

[cor-dohn bleugh]

## High quality cooking
(literally, blue ribbon)

# 'Classique ou moderne, il n'y a qu'une seule cuisine . . . La bonne'

## Paul Bocuse

[cla-seek ooh mod-airn-eu, eel nee-ya kewn
kwee-zeen . . . lah bonn-eu]

'It doesn't matter if the cuisine is
classic or modern; all that matters
is that it's good cooking'

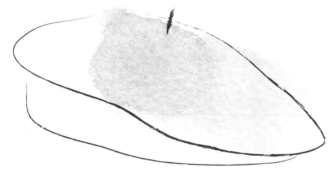

# La Mode

French Style

Simple, understated, elegant yet free-spirited, French style is envied the world over and seemingly impossible to emulate. 'Effortless' is the word most often used to describe it, and indeed it does feel as if the French simply wake up, get dressed and look chic, and yet none of us could do the same.

This chapter celebrates France's love of fashion in all its guises, from the words the French have lent the world to those that describe that elusive allure and je ne sais quoi we're all unsuccessfully seeking to capture.

# Le prêt-à-porter

[luh pret-a-por-tay]

## Ready-to-wear

# La haute couture

[lah oat-coo-tyoor]

Clothing that is designed
or made to order, by hand, from
expensive fabrics
(literally, high sewing)

# Un défilé

[ahn day-fee-lay]

A fashion show

# Le lèche-vitrines

[luh lesh-vee-treen]

Window-shopping

# Être tiré à quatre épingles

[et-reu tee-ray a catr-ay-pahn-gleu]

## To be impeccably dressed
(literally, to be pulled by four safety pins)

# Une tendance

[ewn tahn-dons]

## A trend

# Une tenue

[ewn tuh-new]

## An outfit

# La fripe

[lah freep]

Vintage/second-hand clothes

# Une vraie icône de style

[ewn vray ee-kohne duh steel]

## A true style icon

# Je m'habille en fonction de mes humeurs

[juh ma-beey ohn fonk-syohn duh mez-oo-meur]

I dress according
to my mood

# Un grand couturier

[ahn grahn coo-tyur-ee-ay]

A great fashion designer

# Dévoiler une collection inédite

[day-vwal-ay ewn ko-lek-syohn ee-nay-deet-eu]

## To unveil a new collection

# Une robe à la fois féminine et intemporelle

[ewn rob-eu a lah fwah fem-ee-nene
ay ahn-tom-por-ehl]

A dress that's both
feminine and timeless

# Une silhouette élégante

[ewn see-loo-wet-eu ehl-ay-gohn-teu]

## An elegant figure

# 'La mode se démode, le style jamais'

## Coco Chanel

[lah mod suh day-mod, luh steel zha-may]

'Fashion fades, style remains'